Lerner SPORTS

ALL-STAR SMACKDOWN

JALEN HURTS VS. JOHN ELWAY

WHO WOULD WIN?

JOE STANLEY

Lerner Publications ◆ Minneapolis

Lerner Publications Company
An imprint of Lerner Publishing Group, Inc.
241 First Avenue North
Minneapolis, MN 55401 USA

For reading levels and more information, look up this title at www.lernerbooks.com.

Main body text set in Aptifer Sans LT Pro.
Typeface provided by Linotype AG.

Editor: Anne E. Hill **Designer:** Martha Kranes
Lerner team: Sue Marquis

Library of Congress Cataloging-in-Publication Data

Names: Stanley, Joe, 1975– author.
Title: Jalen Hurts vs. John Elway : who would win? / Joe Stanley.
Other titles: Jalen Hurts versus John Elway
Description: Minneapolis : Lerner Publications , 2026. | Series: Lerner sports. All-star smackdown | Includes bibliographical references and index. | Audience: Ages 7–11 | Audience: Grades 2–3 | Summary: "Between them, NFL quarterbacks Jalen Hurts and John Elway have three Super Bowl appearances and careers full of highlights. But which quarterback was better? Explore their stats and greatest moments and decide for yourself"— Provided by publisher.
Identifiers: LCCN 2024051412 (print) | LCCN 2024051413 (ebook) | ISBN 9798765668535 (library binding) | ISBN 9798765683460 (paperback) | ISBN 9798765676059 (epub)
Subjects: LCSH: Hurts, Jalen, 1988-—Juvenile literature. | Elway, John, 1960-—Juvenile literature. | Quarterbacks (Football)—Juvenile literature.
Classification: LCC GV939.H865 S73 2026 (print) | LCC GV939.H865 (ebook) | DDC 796.332092 [B]—dc23/eng/20241205

LC record available at https://lccn.loc.gov/2024051412
LC ebook record available at https://lccn.loc.gov/2024051413

Manufactured in the United States of America
2-1013189-53821-8/26/2025

TABLE OF CONTENTS

Introduction
Super Quarterbacks 4

Chapter 1
Football Families 8

Chapter 2
Great Moments 14

Chapter 3
Compare the Stats 19

Chapter 4
And the Winner Is 24

Smackdown Breakdown. 28
Glossary. 30
Learn More 31
Index 32

John Elway

INTRODUCTION

SUPER QUARTERBACKS

Denver Broncos quarterback John Elway refused to be stopped at the 1998 Super Bowl. His team lined up at the Green Bay Packers' 12-yard line. Denver needed six yards for a first down. Elway was determined to get it.

- John Elway played both baseball and football at Stanford University.
- Elway led the Broncos to back-to-back Super Bowl wins in 1998 and 1999.
- Jalen Hurts was a football star at the University of Alabama and the University of Oklahoma.
- Hurts scored 41 rushing touchdowns in his first 62 NFL games.

He stepped back and looked for an open wide receiver. But his teammates were all covered by Packers defenders. Elway had no choice but to run. Near the five-yard line, he leaped. He crashed into three Packers players. He spun in the air and landed for a first down. The great play led to a Denver touchdown.

Elway and the Broncos had reached the Super Bowl in 1987, 1988, and 1990. But they lost each time. In 1998, Elway's tough play helped Denver beat Green Bay 31–24. The Broncos were Super Bowl champs for the first time.

Quarterback Jalen Hurts led the Philadelphia Eagles to the big game 25 years later. He did everything he could to

Jalen Hurts

beat the Kansas City Chiefs in the 2023 Super Bowl. Hurts rushed for 70 yards and scored three touchdowns. He passed for 302 yards and threw a touchdown pass. But the Eagles still lost to the Chiefs 38–35.

Elway and Hurts are two great National Football League (NFL) quarterbacks. Elway played in 16 NFL seasons. Hurts is just getting started. But football fans can still compare their stats and skills and choose a favorite. Who will come out on top? Let the smackdown begin!

Hurts throws the ball to an open receiver during the Super Bowl against the Kansas City Chiefs on February 12, 2023.

Elway is carried by two Broncos teammates following their 1998 Super Bowl win over the Green Bay Packers.

CHAPTER 1

John Elway's father, Jack Elway, was a football coach at San Jose State University.

FOOTBALL FAMILIES

John Elway's entire life has centered on football. In 1966, when John was six, he moved with his family to Missoula, Montana. His father was an assistant football coach at the University of Montana. John's father would later become head coach at schools such as San Jose State and Stanford University.

John began playing football in Montana. He loved all sports, including football, baseball, and basketball. He thought about being a running back in football. But his father thought he would be a better fit as quarterback.

John starred as a quarterback at Granada Hills High School in Los Angeles, California. He also led the school's baseball team to the 1979 city championship. Later that year, he started college at Stanford University.

At Stanford, Elway's strong throwing arm made him both a football and baseball star. In 1982, he threw 24 touchdown

Elway (left) was the quarterback at Stanford University in Palo Alto, California.

CONSIDER THIS

The New York Yankees chose Elway in the 1981 Major League Baseball draft. He played pro baseball in 1982 before switching to football full-time.

passes for the football team. He won the Pacific-10 (PAC-10) Conference Player of the Year award for the second time.

In 1983, the Indianapolis Colts chose Elway with the first overall pick in the NFL Draft. But Elway didn't want to play for the Colts. A few days later, the team traded him to the Broncos.

Jalen Hurts has played football for as long as he can remember. Like Elway, Jalen is also the son of a football coach. Jalen grew up in Channelview, Texas. In 2006, when Jalen was eight, his father started coaching the football team at Channelview High School.

With his father as head coach, Jalen played quarterback at Channelview. He also played baseball, but he quit after his freshman year. He wanted to focus on playing football.

Football was the right choice for Jalen. He was a high school junior during the 2014–2015 season. He thew 16 touchdown passes and rushed for 17 touchdowns. He was even better as a senior with 18 passing and 17 rushing touchdowns.

After high school, Hurts attended the University of Alabama. As a freshman in 2016, he threw 23 touchdown passes and scored 13 rushing touchdowns. He wasn't quite as good in 2017 with 17 passing and 8 rushing touchdowns. But he still led Alabama to an 11–1 regular-season record.

Hurts began his college football career at the University of Alabama.

Hurts (right) makes a play against the Auburn Tigers in 2017.

On January 9, 2018, Alabama played in the NCAA championship game. They faced the University of Georgia Bulldogs. Hurts didn't play well. He completed only three passes in the first half. At halftime, Alabama coach Nick Saban replaced Hurts with backup quarterback Tua Tagovailoa. Tagovailoa led Alabama to a comeback win.

The next season, Hurts was Tagovailoa's backup. Then, in 2019, Hurts transferred to the University of Oklahoma. He had his best season yet. He threw 32 touchdowns with only eight interceptions. He was ready for the NFL. The Eagles chose him in the second round of the 2020 draft.

Hurts looks for an open wide receiver during an Eagles practice.

CHAPTER 2

Elway warms up before the 1987 AFC Championship game against the Cleveland Browns.

GREAT MOMENTS

John Elway's leaping, spinning first down in the 1998 Super Bowl was one of many great plays in his career. He never gave up during games. Even if his team was losing, Elway often found a way to lead them to victory.

Elway's first comeback win came in his very first NFL season. The Broncos trailed the Colts 19–0 in the fourth quarter of a 1983 game. Elway and his teammates kept fighting. He threw three touchdown passes to give Denver a 21–19 victory.

Elway continued to lead comebacks in the following seasons. In 1985, he led the Broncos to an amazing seven comeback wins. But his greatest comeback of all time might have been the AFC Championship game on January 11, 1987. The winner of the game between the Broncos and the Cleveland Browns would play in the Super Bowl.

Elway (right) tries to evade linebacker Chip Banks of the Cleveland Browns (center).

The Broncos were in a tough spot. They trailed by seven points with less than six minutes left in the game. Even worse, they had the ball on their own two-yard line. They would have to drive the ball 98 yards to score.

Elway led the way. In 15 plays, he drove the Broncos down the field. With just 39 seconds on the game clock, he threw a touchdown pass to wide receiver Mark Jackson. Denver tied the game and won in overtime.

Elway (left) threw for 244 yards and a touchdown in the AFC Championship game against the Browns.

Hurts runs with the football during the 2023 NFC Championship game versus the 49ers.

Jalen Hurts hasn't played as long as Elway did. But Hurts already has some amazing NFL moments. The biggest game of his career so far was on January 29, 2023. The Eagles faced the San Francisco 49ers in the NFC Championship game.

Hurts led his team on three scoring drives in the first half. In the third quarter, he rushed for a touchdown. The score gave his team a 28–7 lead. The 49ers couldn't catch up. The Eagles advanced to the Super Bowl. The final score was 31–7.

CONSIDER THIS

The Eagles should have won the 2023 Super Bowl. Hurts helped them score 35 points. No other team has ever scored that many points and lost the big game.

In the Super Bowl against the Kansas City Chiefs, Hurts did everything he could to win. His 70 rushing yards set a new Super Bowl record. His three rushing touchdowns tied another record. But it wasn't enough to beat the Chiefs. The Eagles lost the championship 38–35.

Hurts throws to an open receiver during the first quarter of the 2023 Super Bowl against the Kansas City Chiefs.

CHAPTER 3

Elway in action during a 1985 game

COMPARE THE STATS

Elway has many incredible stats. His 51,475 career passing yards rank 12th. His 300 career passing touchdowns are 14th on the NFL's all-time list.

Elway had one of the strongest throwing arms in the league. He was a great passer, and he was also a strong runner. He racked up more than 3,000 passing yards and 200 rushing yards in seven straight seasons. He is the only player in NFL history to do this.

Elway's passing and rushing stats are notable. But most fans remember him best for two things: comebacks and Super Bowls. He led the Broncos to 47 fourth-quarter comebacks.

The Broncos lost the 1978 Super Bowl to the Dallas Cowboys. Denver didn't return to the big game until Elway joined the team. He led them to the Super Bowl in 1987, 1988, and 1990. They lost all three games.

Elway (left) gets around 49ers safety Chet Brooks (right) during the 1990 Super Bowl.

Elway prepares to hand off the ball during the 1998 Super Bowl against the Green Bay Packers.

In 1998, Elway and the Broncos returned to the Super Bowl. They beat the Packers for their first NFL title. The next season, Denver faced the Atlanta Falcons in the Super Bowl. This time, the game was no contest.

The Broncos blew out the Falcons 34–19. Elway passed for 336 yards and won the Super Bowl Most Valuable Player award. About three months later, the 38-year-old quarterback retired from playing football.

Hurts throws a pass during the second quarter of the 2023 Super Bowl.

Hurts also has some amazing stats. In 2022, he threw 22 touchdowns and rushed for 13 more. His 35 total touchdowns set a new Eagles record. The next season, he broke his own record with 38 combined touchdowns.

Hurts put all his skills on display at the 2023 Super Bowl. But like Elway, Hurts lost his first try at the NFL title. With his quarterback skills and a strong team around him, Hurts could get another chance at a Super Bowl victory soon.

CONSIDER THIS

Elway scored 33 rushing touchdowns in his 234 NFL games. Hurts has scored an impressive 41 rushing touchdowns in his first 62 NFL games.

Hurts runs the ball during the 2023 Super Bowl.

CHAPTER 4

Elway passes during a 1993 game against the Browns.

AND THE WINNER IS

Who wins this all-star smackdown? Football fans have their own opinions and can make their own choice. Elway and Hurts are both great quarterbacks. Elway played much longer than Hurts has, so it can be hard to compare them. Let's review what we know.

Elway was a great passer and a good rusher. Hurts is great at both passing and rushing. His rushing skills beat Elway's.

Elway (left) with his Super Bowl MVP award and Broncos head coach Mike Shanahan (right) in 1999

Elway was known for comebacks. No one in NFL history was better at leading his team to a come-from-behind victory. Elway also led the Broncos to five Super Bowls and two NFL titles.

Elway is the winner of this quarterback smackdown. Hurts still has time to match Elway's Super Bowl wins. But unless he does, Elway is on top.

What do you think? Do you agree that Elway is the winner? Or do you think Hurts's amazing skills make him the better quarterback? Review the facts, and make your own pick!

Known for his rushing touchdowns, Hurts (center) runs the ball during a game against the Buffalo Bills in 2023.

Elway gives a thumbs-up after leading the Broncos to a 1998 Super Bowl win.

SMACKDOWN BREAKDOWN

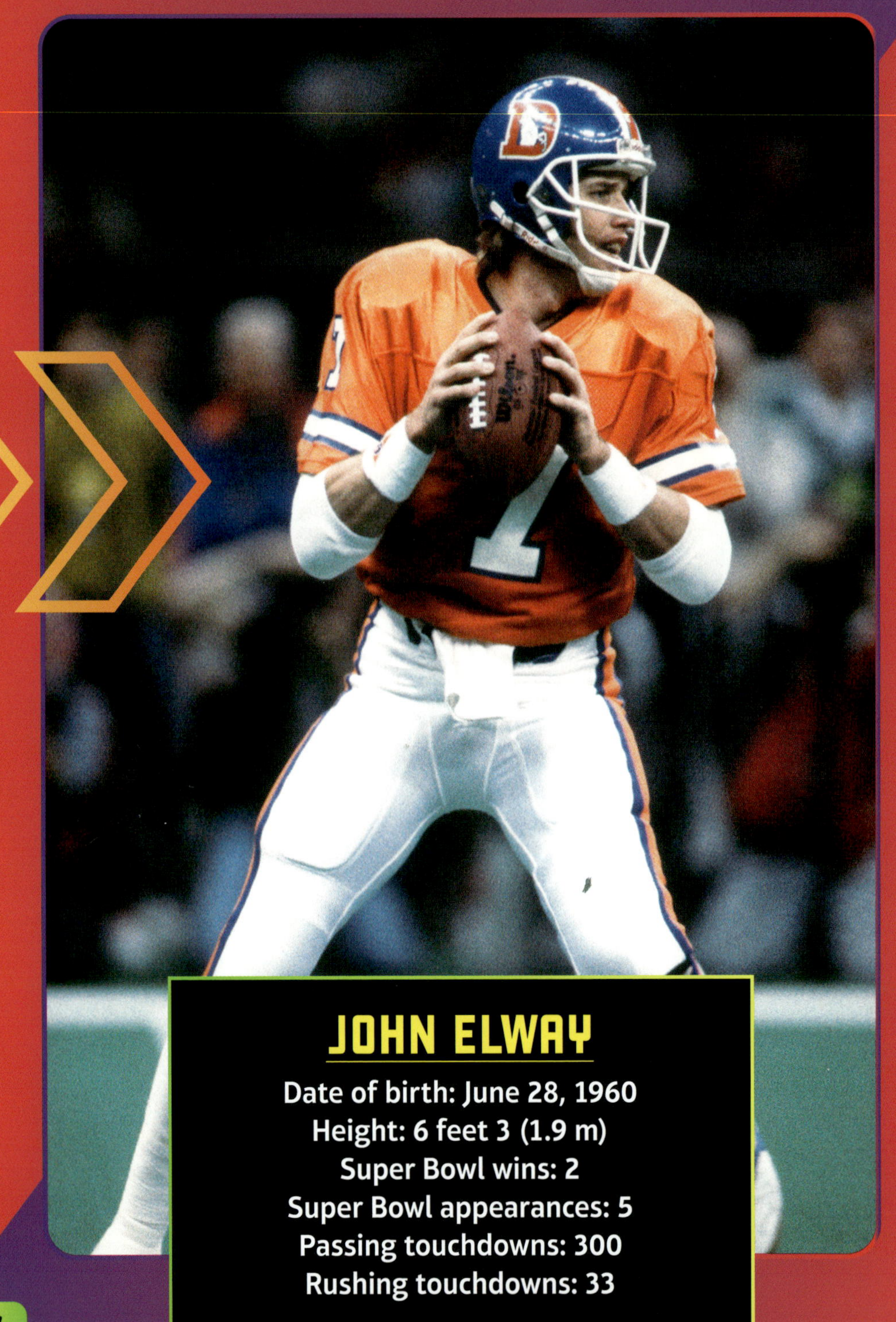

JOHN ELWAY

Date of birth: June 28, 1960
Height: 6 feet 3 (1.9 m)
Super Bowl wins: 2
Super Bowl appearances: 5
Passing touchdowns: 300
Rushing touchdowns: 33

Stats are accurate through the 2023 NFL season.

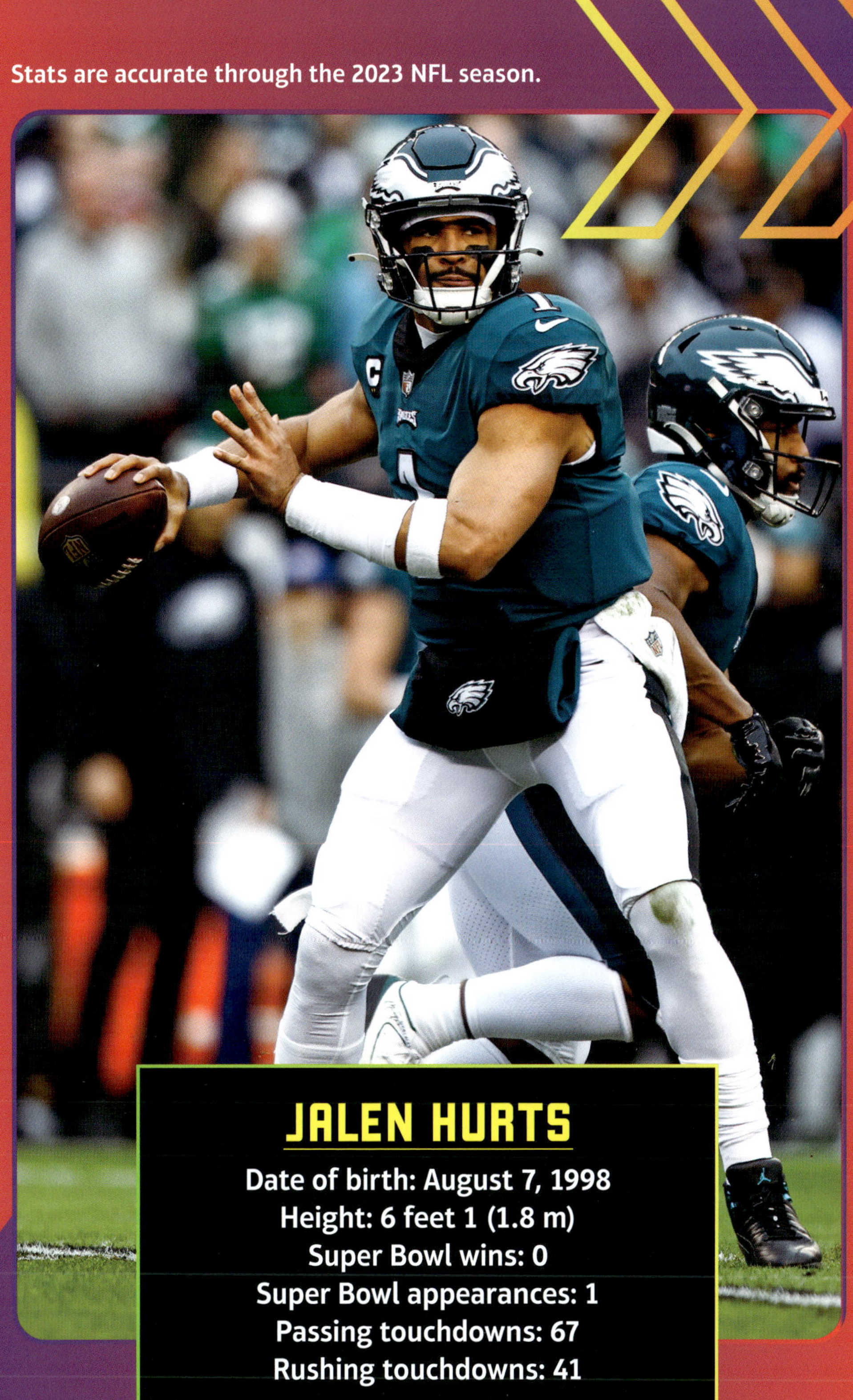

JALEN HURTS

Date of birth: August 7, 1998
Height: 6 feet 1 (1.8 m)
Super Bowl wins: 0
Super Bowl appearances: 1
Passing touchdowns: 67
Rushing touchdowns: 41

GLOSSARY

AFC: American Football Conference

backup: a person who takes the place of or supports another

comeback: to recover after being behind in a game or contest

draft: when teams take turns choosing new players

drive: a series of football plays

interception: a pass caught by the defending team

NCAA: National Collegiate Athletic Association

NFC: National Football Conference

regular season: when all the teams in a league play one another to determine playoff teams

rush: to advance the football by running with it

title: championship

LEARN MORE

Adamson, Thomas K. *Jalen Hurts*. Minneapolis: Bellwether Media, 2024.

Anderson, Josh. *Inside the Denver Broncos*. Minneapolis: Lerner Publications, 2024.

Ducksters: National Football League
https://www.ducksters.com/sports/national_football_league.php

Kiddle: Denver Broncos Facts for Kids
https://kids.kiddle.co/Denver_Broncos

Kiddle: Philadelphia Eagles Facts for Kids
https://kids.kiddle.co/Philadelphia_Eagles

Lynne, Douglas. Jalen Hurts: NFL Star. Burnsville, MN: Press Room Editions, 2024.

INDEX

Channelview, TX, 10
Cleveland Browns, 15

Dallas Cowboys, 20
Denver Broncos, 4–5, 10, 14–16, 20–21, 26

Indianapolis Colts, 10, 14

Jackson, Mark, 16

Kansas City Chiefs, 6, 18

Los Angeles, CA, 9

Missoula, MT, 8
Major League Baseball draft, 10

New York Yankees, 10

Philadelphia Eagles, 5–6, 12, 17–18, 22

Saban, Nick, 12
San Francisco 49ers, 17
San Jose State University, 8
Stanford University, 4, 8–9

Tagovailoa, Tua, 12

University of Alabama, 4, 11–12
University of Montana, 8
University of Oklahoma, 4, 12

PHOTO ACKNOWLEDGMENTS

Image credits: Focus on Sport/Getty Images, pp. 4, 19, 21, 28; Christian Petersen/Getty Images, pp. 5, 6, 18; Timothy A. Clary/AFP via Getty Images, p. 7; Mickey Pfleger/Sports Illustrated via Getty Images, p. 8; Bettmann/Getty Images, p. 9; Kevin C. Cox/Getty Images, pp. 11, 12; Chris Szagola-Pool/Getty Images, p. 13; George Gojkovich/Getty Images, pp. 14, 15; Tony Tomsic/Sports Illustrated via Getty Images, p. 16; Tim Nwachukwu/Getty Images, p. 17; Paul Spinelli via AP, p. 20; Sarah Stier/Getty Images, p. 22; Gregory Shamus/Getty Images, p. 23; George Gojkovich/Getty Images, p. 24; Rhona Wise/AFP via Getty Images, p. 25; Mitchell Leff/Getty Images, p. 26; Doug Collier/AFP via Getty Images), p. 27; Kevin Sabitus/Getty Images, p. 29.

Cover images: Marty Jean-Louis/Alamy Live News (Hurts); Rich Kane Photography/Alamy Stock Photo (Elway).